*Gabriela Popa*

# STRESSFUL DAY, MELT AWAY!

Coloring book

Published in 2015 by
*Pixiphoria*
St. Louis, MO

Copyright © 2015 Gabriela Popa

All rights reserved. No part of this publication may be reproduced or transmitted in any form or by any means, electronic or mechanical, including photocopy, recording or any other information storage and retrieval system, without written permission from the publisher.

ISBN:0983864144
ISBN-13:978-0-983864141

Printed in the United States of America

Date

Location

Author

Date

Location

Author

Date

Location

Author

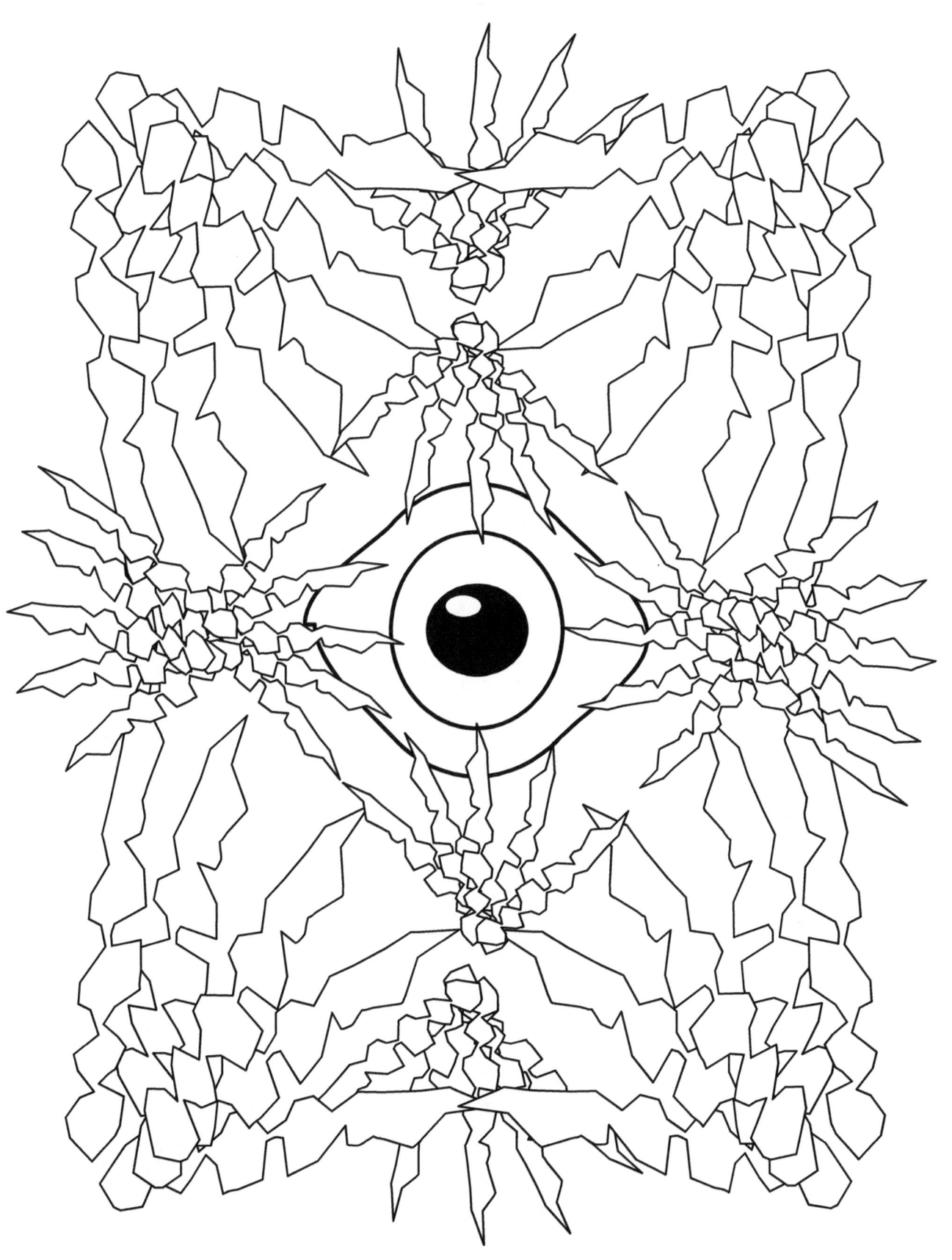

Date _____

Location _____

Author _____

Date

Location

Author

Date

Location

Author

Date

Location

Author

Date
Location
Author

Date
Location
Author

Date

Location

Author

Date

Location

Author

Date
Location
Author

Date

Location

Author

Date

Location

Author

Date

Location

Author

Date
Location
Author

Date

Location

Author

Date
Location
Author

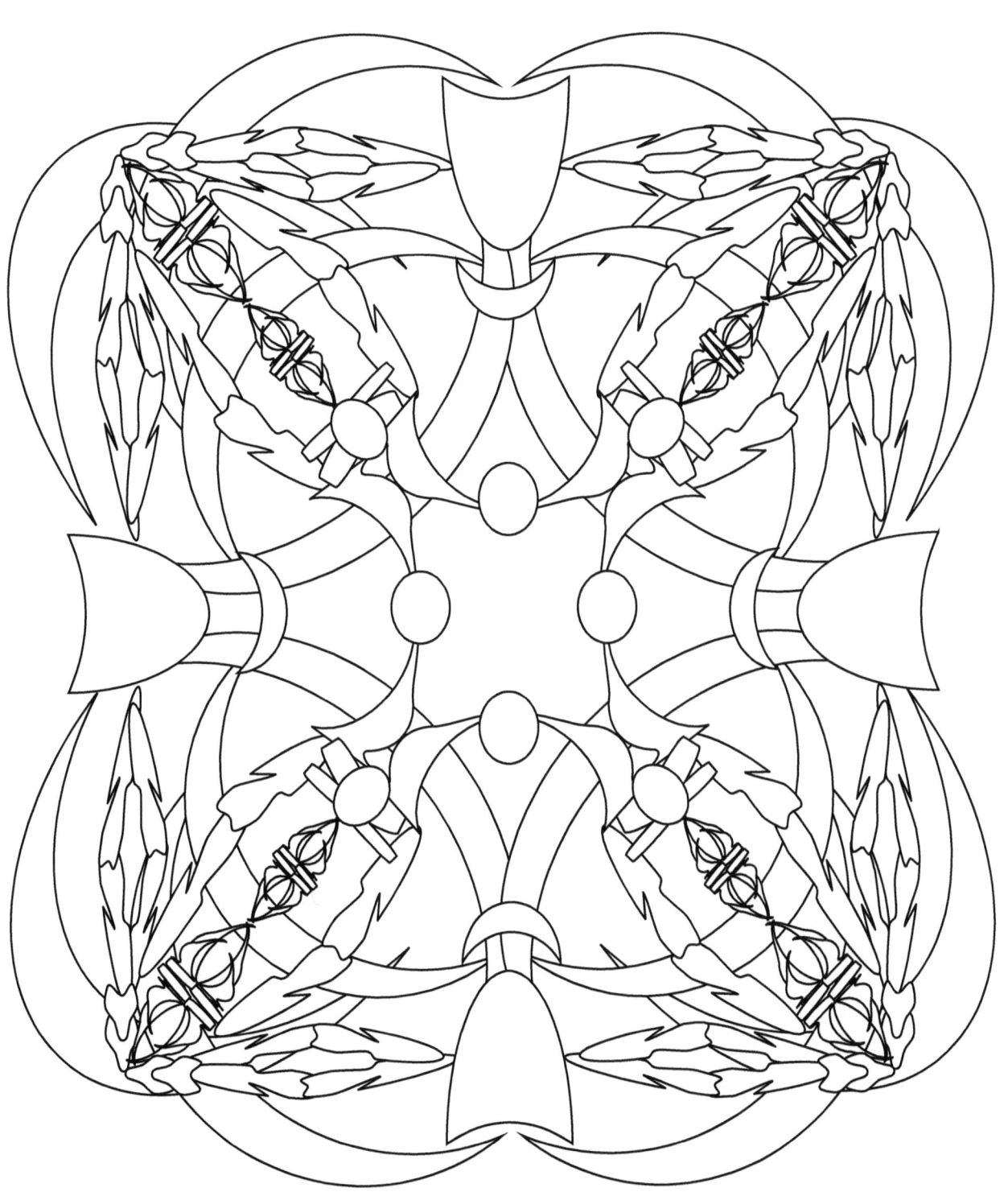

Date

Location

Author

Date
Location
Author

Date
Location
Author

Date

Location

Author

Date

Location

Author

Date
Location
Author

Date

Location

Author

Date

Location

Author

Date
Location
Author

Date
Location
Author

Date

Location

Author

Date

Location

Author

Date

Location

Author

Date
Location
Author

Date
Location
Author

Date

Location

Author

Date

Location

Author

Date

Location

Author

Date

Location

Author

Date
Location
Author

Date

Location

Author

Date
Location
Author

Date

Location

Author

Date
Location
Author

Date
Location
Author

Date
Location
Author

Date

Location

Author

Date
Location
Author

Date

Location

Author

Date

Location

Author

Date
Location
Author

Date

Location

Author

Date

Location

Author

Date

Location

Author

Date

Location

Author

Date
Location
Author

Date

Location

Author

Date
Location
Author

Date
Location
Author

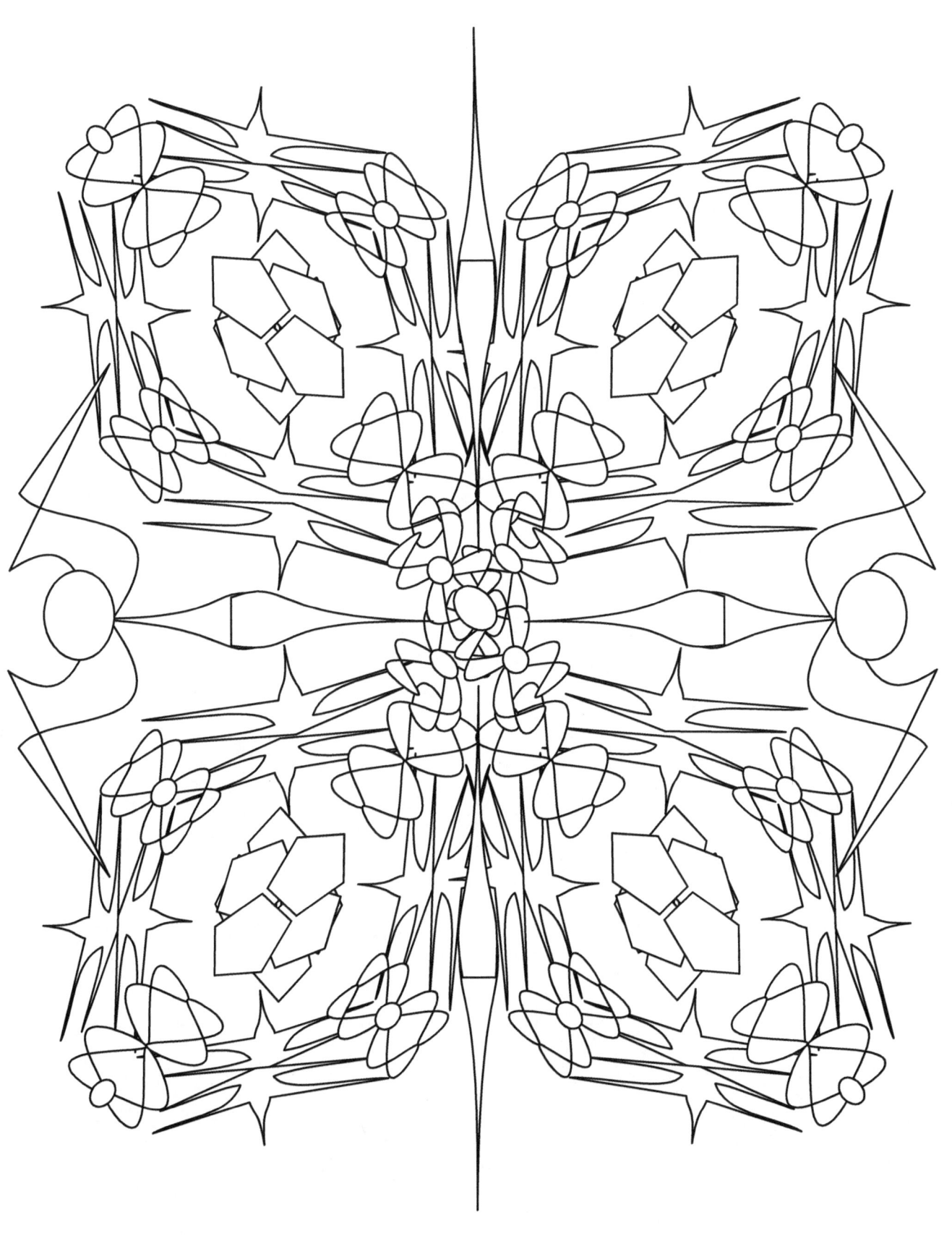

Date
Location
Author

Date

Location

Author

Date

Location

Author

Date

Location

Author

Date
Location
Author

Date

Location

Author

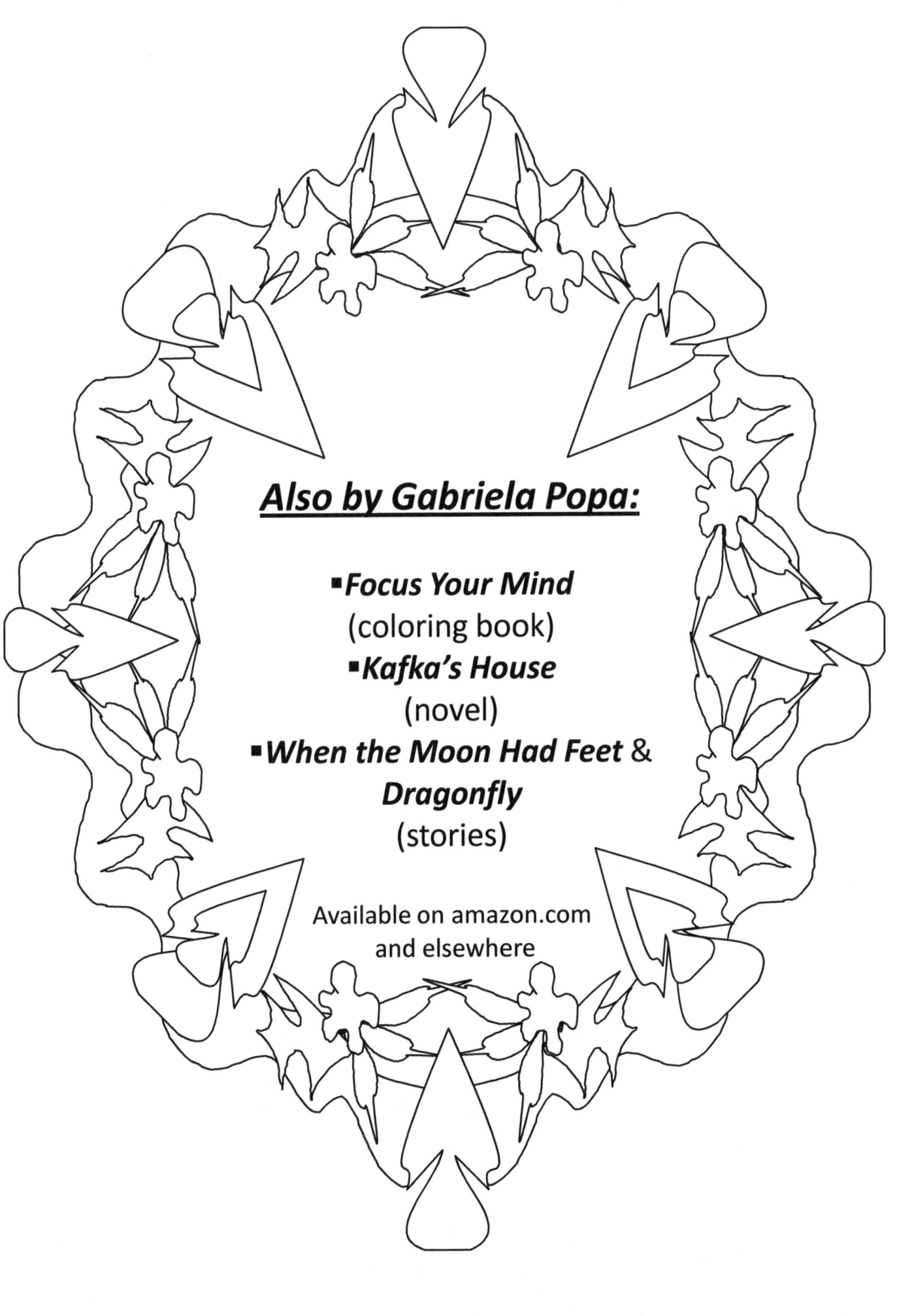

**Also by Gabriela Popa:**

- *Focus Your Mind* (coloring book)
- *Kafka's House* (novel)
- *When the Moon Had Feet* & *Dragonfly* (stories)

Available on amazon.com and elsewhere

www.ingramcontent.com/pod-product-compliance
Lightning Source LLC
LaVergne TN
LVHW061254060426
835507LV00020B/2311